INNOVATORS

Jonathan Ive

Designer of the iPod

Other titles in the Innovators series include:

INNOVATORS

Jonathan Ive
Designer of the iPod

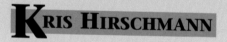

KRIS **H**IRSCHMANN

KIDHAVEN PRESS
An imprint of Thomson Gale, a part of The Thomson Corporation

THOMSON
GALE™

Detroit • New York • San Francisco • New Haven, Conn. • Waterville, Maine • London

For more information, contact
KidHaven Press
27500 Drake Rd.
Farmington Hills, MI 48331-3535
Or you can visit our Internet site at http://www.gale.com

LIBRARY OF CONGRESS CATALOGING-IN-PUBLICATION DATA

Hirschmann, Kris, 1967–
    Jonathan Ive, designer of the iPod / by Kris Hirschmann.
        p. cm. — (Innovators)
    Includes bibliographical references and index.
    ISBN-13 978-0-7377-3533-8 (hardcover : alk. paper)
    ISBN-10 0-7377-3533-3 (hardcover : alk. paper)
    1. Ive, Jonathan, 1967—Juvenile literature. 2. Industrial designers—Biography—Juvenile literature. 3. iPod (Digital music player) 4. Computer engineering. I. Title.
TS140.I94H57 2006
745.2092—dc22
                                                        2006018665

Printed in the United States of America

CONTENTS

Success by Design

Apple Inc. is well known for its **innovative** designs. The iMac, the iBook, the PowerBook, the iPod, and other Apple products are popular not only because they work well, but also because they look great. They combine easy usage and a sense of style in a way that has captured the loyalty of users all over the world.

People may be familiar with Apple's products, but most have never heard of the man most responsible for their creation: As the company's senior vice president of **industrial design**, Jonathan Ive has breathed life into every Apple device since the early 1990s. Working closely with chief executive officer Steve Jobs, Ive and his team pay attention to every detail of every project. They strive to make their designs beautiful as well as functional, and so far they have a remarkable record of success. Starting with the first iMac in 1998, the team has released a string of attractive machines that have amazed the public and stunned the design industry.

In recent years, Ive has received a great deal of recognition for his work. He was named Designer of the Year for 2002 by the Design Museum of London, England. In 2005 he received creative organization D&AD's President's Award for outstanding contribution to the world of creativity. He has also earned awards from many other organizations, including the Industrial Designers Society of America, the German design museums Red Dot and iF, and the (UK) Royal Society of Arts. His work is displayed in museums all over the world, including the Museum of Modern Art in New York City and the Pompidou Center in

Jonathan Ive and his team at Apple helped design the revolutionary iPod.

Paris, France. His name regularly shows up on the "most influential" lists that magazines love to compile.

Ive's work has even been noted by Britain's royal family. On December 30, 2005, the British-born designer was awarded the title of Commander of the Most Excellent Order of the British Empire (CBE) by Queen Elizabeth II. Just one step below knighthood, the CBE title recognizes Ive's work in the field of industrial design. It is a fitting honor for a man who thought he was just doing his job, but who accidentally changed several industries instead. Ive has single-handedly proved that good design can make a real difference—and in the end, that truth may turn out to be this innovator's most important **legacy.**

CHAPTER 1

A Developing Talent

Jonathan Ive was born in 1967 in London, England. Today Ive does not talk much about his childhood, but it is known that his father worked as a silversmith, then a teacher, then a government inspector for design and technology programs in schools. All these jobs involved design in some way. Growing up with this role model, it is not surprising that Jonathan became interested in design. Through play and study, he spent his childhood and young adulthood learning the skills that would eventually make him one of the world's top industrial designers.

Interested in Objects

At a very young age, Jonathan started taking apart radios, cassette recorders, and clocks. He wanted to see what was inside and to figure out how the devices worked. "The fact they had been designed was not obvious or even interesting to me initially,"[1] Ive recalls.

Flowers bloom in Northumbria, England, where Jonathan Ive studied at Newcastle Polytechnic.

After a while, though, Jonathan's focus shifted. The young man started to pay more attention to products' shapes, materials, and other design-related features. He became more and more interested in the way things had been made as well as the way they worked. By the time Jonathan was thirteen or fourteen years old, he knew he wanted to turn his interest into a career, so he started to take art and design classes.

A few years later, Jonathan graduated from secondary school (the UK term for high school). His interest in design was stronger than ever, but he knew he needed more education before he could become a working designer. Jonathan looked at different courses but chose product design rather than specializing in a single area such as furniture or car design. Jonathan thus enrolled in Newcastle Polytechnic (now known as Northumbria).

Advanced Education

At Newcastle, Jonathan started to learn the basics of professional design work. He studied form and color, and he learned how these features affect the way people think of objects. He learned about **manufacturing**, which is the physical process of making things. He also started to understand that each product has a historical and cultural **context**. In other words, an object's design is based partly on the design of earlier objects as well as the lifestyles and beliefs of the people who will use it.

Besides learning concepts, Jonathan was also doing hands-on work. In this area, he was an unusually dedicated student.

A Private Person

In person, Jonathan Ive comes across as an ordinary guy. He is soft-spoken and relaxed, with short dark hair and a muscular build. He usually wears jeans, dark T-shirts, and running shoes, even at work. He becomes enthusiastic when he talks about design issues, but otherwise he is not talkative around reporters.

Ive does not like discussing his personal life, but he has revealed a few details over the years. He lives with his wife, Heather, and two sons in a modest house. He likes Aston-Martin automobiles, showing an appreciation for well-designed cars. He also loves music.

He would rework his projects over and over until he felt they were just right. On one final project, Jonathan built a hundred test models when most other students built only five or six.

Jonathan did all this work by hand partly because he could not understand the design-related computer programs that might have helped him. "I went through college having a real problem with computers. I was convinced that I was technically inept, which was frustrating as I wanted to use computers to help me with various aspects of my design,"[2] he remembers.

Just before Jonathan finished college, however, he discovered a computer that was better than any other he had ever used before. It was called the Macintosh, and it changed Jonathan's view not only of computers in general but also of their design. "I remember being astounded at just how much better [the Mac] was than anything else I had tried to use. I was struck by the care

The original Macintosh, known for its all-in-one design, redefined the personal computer in 1984.

taken with the whole user experience. I had a sense of connection via the object with the designers,"[3] Ive says today. Jonathan was impressed that Apple, the California-based company that sold the Macintosh, was doing creative work in an industry not known for originality or attractive design.

The Working World

After graduating from Newcastle Polytechnic in 1989, Ive was invited to work for a London-based company called Tangerine. This company was a **consultancy** that designed consumer products for clients all over the world. At Tangerine, Ive found himself designing everything from hair combs and bathroom sinks to power tools and television sets. In the process, he learned many things about himself. "I worked out what I was good at and what I was bad at. It became pretty clear . . . I was really only interested in design. I was neither interested [in] nor good at building a business,"[4] he says.

During his time at Tangerine, Ive not only learned about himself. He also got an insider's look at the business of design consulting, and he was not very happy with what he saw. Ive discovered that out-of-house designers were almost never included in early discussions about products. This meant that by the time clients contacted Tangerine, they had already made most of the big decisions about a project. The designer was expected to produce exactly what the client wanted rather than putting any creativity into the job. Ive found this role too limiting. The young designer became increasingly unhappy with his work at Tangerine and with design consulting in general.

During this period Ive drove across the country to present an idea for a new toilet to one of Tangerine's clients. Because the meeting took place on a national comedy-support day, the firm's head of marketing wore a red clown nose throughout the meeting. He half-listened to the things Ive said, then rejected his designs. Ive left the meeting feeling disrespected and discouraged. He started to think that there must be a better way to use his design talents.

A New Opportunity

Shortly after the disastrous meeting, Ive traveled to Cupertino, California. He was scheduled to make a presentation at Apple Computer, the company whose innovative designs he had admired during his college days. Apple had hired Ive to come up with ideas for a new laptop computer.

In California, Ive showed his work to high-ranking Apple executives. The executives were so pleased with what they saw that they asked Ive to work full-time for Apple. He would be in charge of the department that designed computers and computer-related products. It was a big job with a lot of responsibility, and Ive—then just twenty-five years old—was not sure he was ready for it. "I still remember Apple describing this fantastic opportunity and being so nervous that I would mess it all up,"[5] he recalls today.

Despite his nervousness, Ive was interested in Apple's offer. He liked the idea of coming up with design ideas himself instead of polishing other people's ideas as an outside consultant. He thought he might have the chance to be truly creative if he worked for Apple. "It's difficult to do something radically new, unless you are at the heart of a company,"[6] he explains. With this idea in mind, Ive accepted the job at Apple. He made the move to California's **Silicon Valley** in 1992, feeling excited and upbeat about his new role.

A Brief History of Apple

Apple Computer, Inc., was founded in 1976 by Steve Jobs and Steve Wozniak. Early Apples were just like every other computer being sold at the time. To operate them, users had to type in complicated strings of text. In the early 1980s, however, Jobs became convinced that computers should use image-based **graphical user interfaces (GUIs)** instead of text. The wildly successful Apple Macintosh, which was released in 1984, was the first personal computer to feature this technology.

Soon after the Mac was launched, Jobs left Apple. The company did well without him for many years and became known for its innovative products. In the early 1990s, though, things started to change. Sales of Windows-based computers were climbing, and Apple's sales were falling as a result. Little by little the company stopped trying to be creative and started copying its competitors. But this strategy did not work. Apple's sales kept dropping, and industry observers said the company had lost its edge.

In 1997, Apple bought NeXT, the business that Jobs had created after he left Apple in 1985. Jobs was a part of Apple again, and the company's board of directors did not intend to let his talents go to waste. They asked Jobs to be the company's chief executive officer. Jobs agreed—and the company's remarkable turnaround began.

Apple cofounders Steve Jobs (left) and Steve Wozniak (right) flank CEO John Sculley as they show off the Apple IIc computer in 1984.

The eMate was designed by Jonathan Ive and the Apple Design team and released in March 1997. It was made specifically for use in schools, where Apple has long had a strong presence.

A Disappointing Beginning

Ive's enthusiasm faded quickly, however. As an Apple insider, the young designer discovered that the company was no longer doing the original work on which it had built its reputation. The company's top executives were not committed to creativity, and they were too nervous to try new things. This meant that while Ive was technically in charge of Apple's design department, he was still expected to do exactly what his bosses told him to do. "I was certainly closer to where the decisions were being made, but I was only marginally more effective or influential than I had been as a consultant,"[7] Ive remembers today.

This frustrating situation lasted for five years. During this time, Ive did oversee the design of several well-received products, including the Apple Newton personal digital assistant and the eMate **laptop** computer. Still, Ive was not happy with his job. But Jonathan stayed with Apple during hard times, despite interesting outside offers. He believed in the brand and the company.

Everything changed in 1997. In that year Apple cofounder Jobs, who had left the organization in 1985, rejoined the company as chief executive officer. He immediately began to bring back the old values that had once made Apple so successful. Creativity, originality, and innovation were no longer forbidden. Instead they were encouraged and even demanded. It was an atmosphere in which practically anything was possible—and as the company's head of design, Ive was in the perfect position to make exciting things happen.

CHAPTER 2

Breakthrough

When Jobs returned to Apple in 1997, he made product design one of his top priorities. He was particularly interested in moving away from what he called the "beige box" computer model. This clunky design style had worked for the Apple Macintosh and other earlier devices, but Jobs felt that it was time for a change.

To make the change happen, Jobs turned to Ive. He promoted Ive to vice president of industrial design and encouraged him to turn his design talents loose and to find new ways of doing old things. Now a top Apple executive himself, Ive went right to work on these tasks.

A New Breed of Computer

Ive's first assignment was to come up with a personal computer that would be sold mostly to consumers rather than to businesses. For the new device, Jobs wanted to return to the all-in-one monitor and computer design that had made the Apple

Macintosh so popular. But he also wanted the machine to have a totally updated look and feel. It was Ive's job to come up with a design that met both these requirements.

Ive and his design team immediately started to brainstorm with Jobs. They talked and talked about the new machine, asking each other questions like, "How do we want people to feel about it?" and "What part of our minds should it occupy?"[8] They knew that many people were not comfortable with computers, so they decided right away that the new machine should have a simple shape. This would make it seem friendly instead of technical. They also wanted the computer to look more alive, so they decided to build it from smooth, curved plastics instead

Box-shaped Apple Macintosh computers roll off the assembly line in 1984.

The original iMac, launched in August 1998, became a design icon, influencing not just the computer industry, but many other products and even architecture.

of industrial-looking materials. Most important of all, they wanted the device to be extremely easy to use. Every part of the machine, from buttons and plugs to the mouse and keyboard, would be designed with the user's enjoyment in mind.

Once these basic decisions had been made, Ive and his team plunged into the actual work of designing and building the new computer. For ten hectic months they created **prototype** after prototype, making sure they got every detail exactly right. It was a huge job, but little by little, everything got done. By 1998, Apple was ready to release the product that would show the world what Ive and his team could do.

iMac Revealed

The new computer, which was named the iMac G3 or simply the iMac, was revealed to the public on May 7, 1998. The device's design was unlike anything the computer industry had ever seen. Its shape was rounded, almost egglike, instead of boxy like that of other computers. The device was smooth and sleek, with remarkably few slots or holes visible on its outer surface. Most unusual of all, the iMac's shell was transparent in places. This meant that users could look right into their computers and see what was inside.

The see-through shell showed people more than just the guts of their computers. It also gave them a glimpse of Ive's dedication to detail. Ive and his team had designed attractive wires, hardware, and even welding methods to ensure that the inside of the iMac looked just as good as the outside. As Ive said in one interview, "I think—I hope—there's . . . beauty in the internal **architecture** of the product and the way we're fabricating the product. . . . I think that's very important."⁹

Equally important to Ive was the way the iMac's **peripherals** looked. The design team had sweated over the iMac's cables, plugs, keyboard, and other visible parts. One component that got a lot of attention was the iMac's newly designed mouse, which, like its parent computer, was partly transparent. "You see through the Apple logo, like a little window on the top of the mouse, into this little mouse factory. You see the ball moving. . . . It's actually pretty complicated and intriguing,"¹⁰ explains Ive.

Emotional Response

Anyone could see that Ive and his team had created a beautiful object. But making the iMac look good was only one of Ive's goals. The designer also wanted the iMac to make people feel good, and he chose many of the machine's features with this goal in mind.

It Comes in Colors

The original iMac came only in Bondi Blue. The idea of a colorful computer was such a hit, however, that when Apple released an updated iMac in early 1999, it added a fruity rainbow of color options to the package. Buyers could choose among Blueberry, Strawberry, Lime, Tangerine, and Grape. To get the colors just right, Ive consulted with candy makers to find out how they made gumdrops. "Their experience in the science of translucent color control helped us understand [how] to ensure consistency in high volume," remembers Ive.

Quoted in Design Museum, "Jonathan Ive on Apple: iMac—1998," www.designmuseum.org/digital/index.php?pt=2&id=1&des=28.

The iMac line grew to include a wide range of colors.

Color was one tool Ive used. The bottom part of the iMac was formed from **translucent** white plastic. The upper see-through part was a blue green named Bondi Blue after a famous beach in Australia. The color was chosen because Ive and his team thought it would remind people of an inviting ocean on a beautiful summer day. "The Bondi Blue was something that we hoped would be universally appealing,"[11] Ive says today.

The iMac's shape and materials also were chosen partly because of the way they would make people feel. The machine's rounded form was meant to be cute, and the plastic construction was meant to make the device look affordable and toylike. As Ive explains it, "We wanted to make it clear that this isn't a terrifying technology—a technology that still [scares] a huge number of people. . . . We wanted to create this understandable object."[12]

To help consumers reach this understanding, Ive added design touches that made the iMac seem friendly and inviting. He often mentions the carrying handle that he built into the top of the device when explaining this approach. The handle has an obvious function: to help users carry their computers from place to place. Beyond that, says Ive, the handle also tells users something about the way they should feel about the iMac. "Seeing an object with a handle, you instantly understand aspects of its physical nature—I can touch it, move it, it's not too precious,"[13] he explains. Through this detail and others, Ive and his team hoped to make the iMac more appealing to nontechnical people.

Standing Ovation

This strategy turned out to be a roaring success. People did have a few complaints about the machine—they worried about its lack of a floppy disk drive, for instance—but in general, everyone loved the way the new iMac looked. They also liked the feeling it gave them. Thanks in large part to Ive and his team, personal computers did not have to be just functional devices anymore. They could be treasured possessions with a personality all their own. They made people feel comfortable and even affectionate. As Ive put it in one interview, "People want to pat them."[14]

This warm feeling drove sales of the iMac to incredible heights after the machine began shipping in August 1998. Retail stores had sold 800,000 iMacs by the end of the year, easily making the iMac the most popular personal computer on the market at the time. Sales slowed a little bit as time went on, but still, Apple had sold a remarkable 2 million units by August 1999. For the first time in years, the company was keeping up with its competitors. Even more important, it was making a profit—something it had not done in quite some time.

For Ive, though, the greatest reward was not the money but listening to the praise people heaped upon his pet project. Online news service CNET, for example, declared the iMac the most innovative product to hit the consumer market in 1998. The computer also received design awards from *Newsweek*, *Time*, *Popular Science*, *USA Today*, and other media outlets. It

Computer enthusiasts check out the new Apple iMac at a special midnight sale in 1998.

This top view of iMacs shows the handle that served beyond its obvious function. Even people uncomfortable with computers knew what the handle was for and how to use it.

was declared one of the spring's hottest fashion statements by *Vogue* magazine. The positive media response was quite satisfying for Ive and his team, who felt that their hard work was finally getting the recognition it deserved.

It was not only the iMac that was being recognized, however. As the man behind the machine, Ive himself was suddenly attracting a lot of attention. Ive gave interviews and spoke at gatherings to help **publicize** the iMac, but he always seemed uncomfortable in the public eye. He did not like to talk about his personal life, and he absolutely refused to take credit for the iMac's design. He explained to one interviewer, "These projects were very much a team effort, and I wish you could be talking to everyone."[15]

Still, everyone knew that Ive had overseen the development of the iMac, and people felt that he deserved most of the credit. Whether he liked it or not, Ive had become an overnight sensation in the design industry. He was called a genius, and people waited eagerly to see what he would come up with next.

CHAPTER 3

Changing the Computing World

Before the iMac hit the market, Apple had been losing ground against its competitors. The company seemed to have lost its creative edge, and people had stopped taking it seriously. Everything changed after the iMac was introduced. Industry observers saw that Apple was once again producing cutting-edge technology and design, and they were excited. No one knew exactly what the company would do next, but having seen the iMac, everyone was sure it would be revolutionary.

It was up to Ive to fulfill these high expectations. The prospect was daunting. "It's a bit scary,"[16] Ive admitted to a reporter at the time. But Ive and his team soon proved that they were up to the task, producing a number of innovative products from 1999 onward. Some of these products were hits with consumers, while others were downright flops. All, however, featured the stunningly simple design and careful attention to detail that had made the original iMac so popular. Ive's reputation grew steadily as the years went by, and his body of work increased.

Home and Office

Some of Ive's most interesting designs were updates to the iMac G3. These updated machines worked much like the original device, so they were also called iMacs. But in appearance, they were completely different from the original version. The iMac G4, for instance, had an arm-mounted flat-screen monitor that was attached to a rounded base. Looking more like a desk lamp than a computer, the G4 sold briskly from 2002 to 2004. The G5, which replaced the G4 and was still being sold in mid-2006, looks like a large, free-standing screen without any computer attachment at all. The device's hard drives and other working parts are hidden right inside the monitor.

The iMac G4 (left) had a flat LCD display that seemed to "float" in mid-air and was adjustable with just a touch. The iMac G5 (right) built the entire computer into the display and featured an iSight camera for video conferencing.

Team Effort

As Jonathan Ive is quick to point out, every Apple product is designed by a group, not an individual. Ive works with a carefully chosen team of designers that has now been together for many years. In a 2003 interview, Ive described the team and the environment in which it operates:

> We have assembled a heavenly design team. By keeping the core team small and investing significantly in tools and process, we can work with a level of collaboration that seems particularly rare. Our physical environment reflects [this] approach. The large open studio and massive sound system support a number of [shared] design areas. We have little . . . personal space. In fact, the memory of how we work will endure beyond the products of our work.

Quoted in Design Museum, "Jonathan Ive: Designer of the Year 2003," www.designmuseum.org/design/index.php?id=63.

Other consumer models Ive designed include the eMac, which was launched in 2002, and the Mac Mini, which became available in 2005. As of mid-2006, both of these devices were still on the market. The eMac is similar in shape to the original iMac G3 and is sold mostly to schools. The Mac Mini, an extremely powerful computer that needs to be hooked up to a separately purchased monitor, looks like a small metallic box with rounded edges. It takes up less desk space than a box of tissues.

Ive's signature style also showed up in computers created mainly for the business market. The PowerMac G3, G4, and G5 resembled typical computer towers, but they were far from typical in their attention to detail. Demonstrating the PowerMac G5 at a press conference in 2003, Ive excitedly showed off some of the machine's fine points. "The care that went into just the door was just extraordinary," he boasted as he removed the case's side panel. "Just check out the hardware we used. Look at the finish and the materials. . . . Look at the detail, but so simple."[17]

Ive is clearly delighted with his creations—and users are, too. Most Ive-designed computers have been commercially successful. The only real exception has been the PowerMac G4 Cube, an almost featureless computer-containing box that was created with professional users in mind. Although the device's design wowed industry observers, the product never caught on with the buying public. Launched in 2000, it was taken off the market after just one year.

On the Road

Ive and his team did not design computers only for the home and office. They also produced many portable computers, which are commonly known as laptops. The team's first effort in this area was the iBook G3, which was launched in 1999. Like the iMac, the iBook was unlike anything else on the market at the time. It was colorful, and it had cute rounded edges. It was also extremely powerful and had a larger screen than any other laptop on the market. Between its appealing looks and its strong performance, the laptop was an instant hit with consumers. It also became a popular prop for TV and movie directors, who often showed stylish characters using iBooks.

Besides the iBook, Ive and his team also designed the Power-Book series, which was created with professional users in mind. Razor thin and light for traveling convenience, Ive's PowerBooks had widescreen monitors so users could easily display two pages side by side. This useful feature was carried over into the Mac-Book Pro, Apple's later entry in the laptop market.

As with every Apple product, Ive paid attention to each detail of his laptop designs. The iBook, for example, has a light that

Apple's notebook computers come with a cord that disconnects easily to limit damage to the machine.

goes on when the device enters standby mode. Instead of shining steadily or blinking on and off, however, the light throbs gently, as if the machine is drawing gentle breaths while it sleeps. Another interesting detail is the power cord of the MacBook Pro. The cord is attached to the computer by a magnetic plug. Under normal conditions, the plug clings tightly to the device's power port. If someone trips over the cord, however, the plug pulls loose easily. By doing this, it prevents the laptop from being accidentally yanked off a desk or another raised surface.

Form Follows Function

There is no doubt that features like throbbing lights and magnetic plugs add style and zing to Ive's products. But Ive is quick to point out that being "cool" is not the ultimate goal of his designs. He wants everything he creates to be simple and useful, and he makes all his decisions with this in mind. By designing products in such a way that technical details are invisible to the end user, says Ive, "What you and I are left to deal with are the things we care about. All of the stuff that makes this technology possible is resolved in a way that doesn't force you to deal with it."[18]

"Find Me an Ive"

Jonathan Ive's success at Apple has changed the way companies approach their design efforts. In a 2005 interview, design recruiter RitaSue Siegel explained the shift.

It used to be that everyone wanted to work in a consultancy . . . because that's where there was variety and the best designers. That's not true anymore. You have just as good designers working inside companies. . . .

In the past two years, more companies have come to us asking for a [vice president] of design or a creative/design director who can give them a personality—an instantly recognizable [look] for their products. They actually say, 'Find me a Jonathan Ive.'

Quoted in Danielle Sacks, "Be the Next Jonathan Ive," *Fast Company*, June 2005, p. 94.

Jonathan Ive in an onstage discussion for students at University of the Arts London, November 2006.

This approach makes Apple's products extremely easy to use. Ive's goal, in fact, is to create things that people can operate without ever looking at an instruction book. Ive and his team are so good at this that they make it look easy. But that is not the case, says Ive. "So much of what we try to do is get to a point where . . . you think 'Of course it's that way, why would it be any other way?' It looks so obvious, but [those solutions are] really hard to achieve,"[19] he explains.

Keeping things simple may be hard, but it gets great results. Today Apple enjoys a reputation for putting out products that make sense from the moment they are turned on. As a result, many people are enthusiastically devoted to the company. When these people need to buy a new computer-related product, they go straight to Apple without even looking at competing devices.

Looks Matter

Other companies cannot avoid noticing Apple's popularity, and many have tried to copy it. Thanks to the influence of Ive and his team, everyday electronics like cell phones, televisions, and answering machines are now available in fancy shapes and colors. Manufacturers hope that these features will add personality to their electronics and make them more appealing to consumers. So far, however, no one has been able to match Apple's success.

It may seem odd that consumers ignore look-alikes and continue to gobble up more expensive Apple equipment. In Jonathan Ive's opinion, it is not strange at all. He is convinced that copycat companies are missing the point. "Being superficially different is the goal of so many of the products we see . . . rather than trying to innovate and genuinely taking the time, investing the resources and caring enough to try and make something better,"[20] he says. In other words, Ive really cares about the objects he designs, and he is committed to making them as good as they can possibly be in every way.

This passion makes Ive stand out among his peers. Today the design industry considers Ive a genius who succeeds brilliantly at everything he does. He is copied, quoted, and consulted—but most of all, he is admired. Ive reminded the world that good design mattered, and he changed the computer industry in the process.

CHAPTER 4

The iPod Revolution

As a designer, Ive is best known for his work in the computer market. In the long term, though, he may be remembered more for his impact on the music industry. As a designer of the iPod MP3 player, Ive has changed not only the way people listen to their favorite songs but the very business of music.

A Simple Idea

The basic idea behind the iPod did not come from Apple. MP3 technology, which **digitized** music by squeezing it into small computer-readable files, had been around since the early 1990s. By the end of the century, MP3 storage devices were being sold to the public. These devices, however, were poorly designed and hard to use. Jobs thought Apple could create a better product, and he asked Ive to prove it.

In response to Jobs's request, Ive and the team at Apple eventually came up with a slim device about the size of a deck of playing cards. The front of the device bore a large round button encircled by four smaller ones. All the device's functions could be operated with these buttons. There was also a screen that showed information about each song's title, artist, and other information while music played. The device was all white, right down to its bud-style earphones. "I remember there was a discussion: 'Headphones can't be white; headphones are black, or dark gray,'"[21] Ive remembers with a chuckle. But Ive felt strongly that the earphones should match the rest of the device, so he insisted upon making them white. Today white earphones have become a symbol of the iPod.

The iPod family, featuring iPod with video; the iPod nano, which is thinner than a no. 2 pencil; and iPod shuffle, the world's smallest MP3 player.

The iPod's looks were important. Even more important, though, was the way the device worked. The iPod's only purpose was to store and play music, and everything about the product was designed to make it easy for people to do that—and only that. The key, explains Ive today, was resisting the temptation to add extra features that might have made the iPod confusing. "Trying to do too much with the device . . . would have been its complication and, therefore, its demise," Ive says. "What's interesting is that out of that simplicity . . . came a very different product. But difference wasn't the goal. . . . [It] was really a consequence of this quest to make [the iPod] a very simple thing."[22]

The iPod Hits the Market

It turned out that the iPod's simplicity appealed to consumers, who started snatching up the device as soon as it hit the shelves in 2001. People liked the iPod because it was easy to use and easy to carry. It held up to a thousand songs, and it let people listen to their favorite music whenever and wherever they liked without the hassle of toting CDs. Even better, the music did not skip when the iPod got jostled. On the road, in the gym, or at home, the iPod was the perfect music delivery system.

The iPod's popularity was helped along by iTunes, an Apple-owned online music store from which iPod users could download CD-quality songs. About 200,000 songs were available through the site, and it cost just 99 cents to download each tune. The online store was an immediate hit with consumers, who loved the idea of buying single songs instead of entire albums. As time went by and the iTunes catalog grew, more and more people chose iPods so they could take advantage of the site's offerings.

Launched in April 2003 with over 200,000 songs sold for 99 cents each, the iTunes Store has grown to include podcasts, music videos, TV shows, feature films and millions more songs.

Meanwhile, other manufacturers did their best to copy Apple's success. Sony, Samsung, SanDisk, and other companies released MP3 players that were less expensive than the original iPod. None of these players worked as well as the iPod, and none of them could hook up to iTunes. As a result, the competition had very little effect on sales of the iPod.

A Huge Hit

More than 100 million iPods had been sold by April 2007. Along the way, people had become so comfortable with the iPod that Apple felt it could add some new features. The basic line offered models with color screens, video players, and digital photo organizers. Each model came in a range of prices. Lower-priced models had less memory, and higher-priced models had more. This flexibility was great for buyers, who now had a choice about how much storage space they could buy and how much money they wanted to spend.

Celebrities Love It

High-profile celebrities regularly praise the iPod. Talk-show host Oprah Winfrey, for example, lists the device as one of her favorite things. Bono, the lead singer of the rock band U2, has called the iPod the most beautiful object in music since the electric guitar. And musician Moby cannot seem to say enough good things about the product. He has talked about it in many interviews and was even featured in an Apple promotional movie.

Even President George W. Bush is a fan. According to a 2005 article, "[Bush] has owned the personal accessory of the moment for some time. He's loaded his iPod with his favorite country singers: George Jones, Kenny Chesney and Alan Jackson. He also listens to Aaron Neville, Creedence and Van Morrison."

Robin Abcarian, "The Bushes Do Culture Their Own Way," *Free New Mexican*, February 16, 2005, www.freenewmexican.com/news/10599.html.

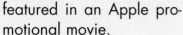

Singer Bono of U2, pictured behind Steve Jobs, has the highest praise for the wildly successful iPod.

Besides the basic device, Ive and his team had also designed a smaller and less expensive version of the iPod. Called the iPod nano, this device is thinner than a pencil and is best known for holding 1,000 songs for $199. Even smaller was the iPod shuffle, which was no larger than a pack of gum. A newer version of the player was smaller still. About the size of a postage stamp, it held 240 songs and cost just $79.

Consumers loved having so many choices, and they continued to love the beautifully simple design of the iPod line. There were countless MP3 players on the market, but none of these products made people feel the same way the iPod did, and they did not work as well. People kept buying Ive's devices—and they kept buying songs from iTunes, which by mid-2006 had a catalog of 3 million songs. Today available to both Apple and Windows users, the site had logged 1 billion downloads by February 2006. A few months later, the site was averaging an incredible 3 million downloads every day.

Changing an Industry

These figures showed how deeply the iPod had shaken up the music industry. Just a few years earlier, record companies had

In February 2006, Apple unveiled the iPod Hi-Fi: an all-in-one, high-fidelity speaker system that delivers room-filling sound.

been suing people for trading music over the Internet. They had vowed that they would not allow this activity to continue. The iPod changed their minds. Music executives realized that people were going to use the device to download music from the Internet, no matter how hard they tried to stop them. By making the process legal, record companies kept a little bit of control over the process and made some money from it, too. Whether they liked it or not, a billion-dollar industry had been born.

This change can be traced back to the iPod and, less directly, to Ive himself. Ive and his team made the iPod beautiful and easy to use, and everything else grew from that point. The industry-shaking impact was not intentional—but it is impossible to deny the results of Ive's efforts. This fact was recognized in 2004, when a poll of music industry experts named Ive and Jobs jointly as the second most powerful people in the music business.

In interviews today, Ive seems a bit stunned by this high praise. Always modest, he shies away from questions about himself, and he refers constantly to the team effort that went into the design of the iPod. Ive lights up, however, when reporters ask him about the way the iPod has affected people's lives. "What's really great is when you talk to a friend or [when] someone you don't know comes up and wants to talk about what the iPod meant for them. That's really fantastic,"[23] he says. He is delighted partly because he knows just how these people feel. Ive himself carries an iPod everywhere he goes and says the device is one of his all-time favorite creations.

Beyond the Music

Ive and the rest of the world will have even more reasons to like the iPod in the future. The device is becoming much more than

The Nike+iPod Sport Kit is a wireless system that transmits information from a running shoe to the iPod nano, which displays information on the screen and plays messages for the user.

a music player. It can now be a mini TV or a digital photo album. It can hold an entire encyclopedia. It can even collect data from computerized Nike running shoes to log a user's workout. Cell phones that use iPod technology are being developed, iPod cradles are now a standard gadget in certain hotel chains, and countless clothing designers are adding iPod pockets to their pants and shirts. In short, the device is becoming a must-have part of people's everyday lives.

Ive's computers, too, will continue to have an impact. They will likely not have as much of an impact as the iPod has had, but they will make a daily difference in the lives of the people who use them. And if history is any indication, future models will continue to dazzle the design world. Ive cannot resist the urge to innovate, which means that his work will always feature something new and exciting. And Ive still has a long career ahead of him, so there is no telling what heights he might achieve in the future.

NOTES

Chapter 1: A Developing Talent

1. Quoted in Design Museum, "Jonathan Ive: Designer of the Year 2003," www.designmuseum.org/design/index.php?id-63.
2. Quoted in Design Museum, "Jonathan Ive: Designer of the Year 2003."
3. Quoted in Design Museum, "Jonathan Ive: Designer of the Year 2003."
4. Quoted in Design Museum, "Jonathan Ive: Designer of the Year 2003."
5. Quoted in Design Museum, "Jonathan Ive: Designer of the Year 2003."
6. Quoted in Caroline Frost, "Jonathan Ive: Apple of the iMac," BBC News, January 18, 2002, http://news.bbc.co.uk/1/hi/in_depth/uk/2000/newsmakers/1768724.stm.
7. Quoted in Design Museum, "Jonathan Ive: Designer of the Year 2003."

Chapter 2: Breakthrough

8. Quoted in Jennifer Tanaka, "No More 'Beige Boxes,'" *Newsweek*, May 18, 1998, p. 48.
9. Quoted in Marcus Fairs, "Jonathan Ive," *Icon*, July/August 2003, www.icon-magazine.co.uk/issues/july-august/ive.htm.
10. Quoted in Dike Blair, "Bondi Blue," *Purple #2*, Winter 1998–1999, www.thing.net/~lilyvac/writing25.html.
11. Quoted in Dike Blair, "Bondi Blue."
12. Quoted in Dike Blair, "Bondi Blue."
13. Quoted in Design Museum, "Jonathan Ive: Designer of the Year 2003."

14. Quoted in Martha Mendoza, "iMac Designer Mixes Creativity, Computing," Cincinnati.com, April 16, 1999, www.cincin nati.com/technology/041699_imac.html.
15. Quoted in Dike Blair, "Bondi Blue."

Chapter 3: Changing the Computing World

16. Quoted in Kristi Essick, "The Man Behind iMac," CNN.com, September 22, 1998, edition.cnn.com/TECH/computing/98 09/22/imacman.idg.
17. Quoted in Leander Kahney, "Design According to Ive," *Wired News*, June 25, 2003, www.wired.com/news/mac/0,2125, 59381,00.html.
18. Quoted in David Derbyshire, "His Goal Was to Make It Simple to Use and a Joy to Look At," Telegraph.co.uk, November 19, 2005, www.telegraph.co.uk/news/main.jhtml?xml=/news/ 2005/11/19/nive19.xml.
19. Quoted in Marcus Fairs, "Jonathan Ive."
20. Quoted in Design Museum, "Jonathan Ive: Designer of the Year 2003."

Chapter 4: The iPod Revolution

21. Quoted in Rob Walker, "The Guts of a New Machine," *New York Times Magazine*, November 30, 2003, http://robwalker. net/contents/as_guts.html.
22. Quoted in Rob Walker, "The Guts of a New Machine."
23. Quoted in David Derbyshire, "His Goal Was to Make It Simple to Use and a Joy to Look At."

GLOSSARY

architecture: The way a computer's parts are built and organized.

consultancy: A business agency that provides professional advice or services to another company.

context: The conditions under which a thing occurs.

digitized: Data changed into a digital (computer-readable) format.

graphical user interfaces (GUIs): Computer programs that let people use a mouse to choose from menus or icons.

industrial design: The design of products intended to be mass produced for the consumer market.

innovative: Featuring original ideas or new ways of doing old things.

laptop: A small personal computer that is designed to be carried around by the user.

legacy: Something that remains important long after it is created.

manufacturing: The physical process of making objects.

peripherals: Devices connected to a computer. Peripherals add extra features or help users communicate with their computers.

prototype: A hand-built model of a computer or a computer part. Prototypes are used to finalize details before a device goes into production.

publicize: To bring something to the attention of the public.

Silicon Valley: An area near San Francisco, California, that is world famous for its many high-tech businesses.

translucent: Allowing some light to shine through, but not transparent.

For Further Exploration

Books

Scott Kelby, *The iPod Book: Doing Cool Stuff with the iPod and the iTunes Music Store.* Berkeley, CA: Peachpit, 2005. This book is written for adults, but it is simple enough for kids to understand. Easy text and full-color pictures explain how to get the most out of the iPod and the iTunes store.

Bill Slavin, *Transformed: How Everyday Things Are Made.* Toronto: Kids Can, 2005. Learn how baseballs, CDs, dental floss, ice cream, and many other products are manufactured. Detailed color illustrations help explain each step in the creation of sixty-nine everyday objects.

Brian Williams, *Great Inventions: Computers.* Chicago: Heinemann Library, 2001. This book examines the invention of the computer and the device's effects on society.

Chris Woodford, *Cool Stuff and How It Works.* New York: Dorling Kindersley, 2005. X-rays and other high-tech methods are used to look inside the iPod and other devices. Includes a technology timeline, bios of groundbreaking inventors, and a glossary of technological terms.

Web Sites

Apple Computer (www.apple.com.). Check out all of Jonathan Ive's designs on Apple's official Web site.

Design Museum (www.designmuseum.org). The London Design Museum interviewed Jonathan Ive on many different subjects when it named him Designer of the Year in 2002. Read these interviews on the Design Museum's Web site.

iTunes (www.apple.com/iTunes). This is the spot to download music for the iPod.

INDEX

PICTURE CREDITS

ABOUT THE AUTHOR

Kris Hirschmann, whose very first computer was an Apple Macintosh, has written more than 130 books for children. She owns and runs The Wordshop (www.theword-shop.com), a business that provides a variety of writing and editorial services. She holds a bachelor's degree in psychology from Dartmouth College in Hanover, New Hampshire.

Hirschmann lives just outside Orlando, Florida, with her husband, Michael, and her daughters, Nikki and Erika.